PHILOSOPHERS OF THE SPIRIT

SOCRATES

PHILOSOPHERS OF THE SPIRIT

SOCRATES

———◆———

Edited by
Robert Van de Weyer

Hodder & Stoughton
LONDON SYDNEY AUCKLAND

Copyright © 1997 Robert Van de Weyer

First published in Great Britain 1997.

The right of Robert Van de Weyer to be identified as the Editor of this
Work has been asserted by him in accordance with the
Copyright, Designs and Patents Act 1988.

1 3 5 7 9 10 8 6 4 2

British Library Cataloguing in Publication Data:
A record for this book is available from the British Library.

ISBN 0 340 69401 7

Typeset in Monotype Columbus by
Strathmore Publishing Services, London N7.

Printed and bound in Great Britain by
Mackays of Chatham PLC, Chatham, Kent

Hodder and Stoughton Ltd,
A division of Hodder Headline PLC
338 Euston Road, London NW1 3BH

CONTENTS

SERIES INTRODUCTION

The first task of philosophers is to ask questions – the questions which lurk in all our minds, but which, out of fear or confusion, we fail to articulate. Thus philosophers disturb us. The second task of philosophers is to try and answer the questions they have asked. But since their answers are inevitably only partial, philosophers both interest and infuriate us. Their third and most important task is to stimulate and inspire us to ask questions and seek answers for ourselves.

The human psyche or spirit has always been the main – although not the only – focus of philosophy. And inevitably when the psyche is explored, the gap between religion and philosophy rapidly narrows. Indeed for philosophers in the more distant past there was no gap at all, since philosophy was an aspect of theology and even mysticism. Although religious institutions are now quite weak, questions of spiritual philosophy are being asked more keenly and urgently than ever.

This series is an invitation to readers, with no philosophical training whatever, to grapple with the great philosophers of the spirit. Most philosophy nowadays is served in the form of brief summaries, written by commentators. Each of these books contains an introduction to the life and ideas of the philosopher in question. But thereafter the reader encounters the philosopher's original words – translated into modern English. Usually the words are easy to follow; sometimes they are more difficult. They are never dull, always challenging, and frequently entertaining.

INTRODUCTION

In the modern world, both West and East, we have come to accept two quite different and separate approaches to truth. There is the scientific approach, which proceeds by logic and experiment to make objective statements about particular features of the natural world. And there is religion – or, more precisely, mysticism – in which the individual proceeds through various forms of personal discipline to discern spiritual meaning. Some people committed to the scientific approach dismiss the mystical approach as self-delusion; and undoubtedly the scientific approach has by far the greater practical impact on our lives. Yet mysticism of one kind or another continues to be held by most people in surprisingly high regard; and a remarkable number claim to have had religious or mystical experiences.

In Socrates these two approaches to truth, logical and mystical, go together. He was a philosopher, committed to discovering truth through rational thought and debate. Apparently he wrote nothing down; his ideas are contained in dialogues and speeches which were subsequently recorded, mainly by Plato. As one reads these words, one enters the presence of a magisterial intellect, able to chop away falsehood by ruthless argument until some piece of truth remains. His is the voice of the university lecture and seminar, and also the research laboratory. If he were alive today, it is easy to imagine him as a professor of almost any of the modern disciplines, with a chair at one of the most prestigious universities.

Yet this is only half the story. Socrates believed that ultimate truth is spiritual, not material; thus it can only be discerned directly by the soul, and not through the five senses. He was convinced that true philosophers – true seekers after truth – must try to detach themselves from the body, to enable the soul to operate freely. He himself abstained from almost all physical comforts, and endured great poverty, in his quest; and he also made himself indifferent to status and reputation, enduring considerable unpopularity among those whose false wisdom he exposed. Finally, when his enemies tried him and sentenced him to death, he refused to plead for mercy or try to escape, declaring that the philosopher's life is a long preparation for death, when the soul shall finally be released from the body.

This fusion of logic and mysticism in Socrates means that his style is both quite familiar to us, and yet disturbingly different from anything we encounter today. We can happily approve his desire to define his terms precisely, and to take his arguments forward step by step, ensuring that each statement follows clearly from the previous one. We can also approve the poetic flights, when he talks about the region of pure spirit beyond the heavens, or the place of humanity within the cosmos, or the inner soul of the earth in which we live. Yet we are likely to feel uneasy when we realise that the poetry is constructed as a logical argument, and that the logical arguments lead us inexorably to spiritual realms beyond logic. We prefer to keep science and religion in separate boxes; but for Socrates there is only one box – marked Truth.

The point at which this fusion is most striking, and also most disturbing, is his discussion of love. Again, in both West and East there is traditionally a distinction between erotic love, associated with our natural, bodily instincts and desires; and spiritual, selfless love, usually assumed to be divinely inspired. For Socrates love in the spiritual sense is also erotic. He describes in the most vivid terms the madness of being in love with another person, in which that other person appears supremely beautiful. And he explains this as the first step on a path that leads to the perfect divine beauty beyond the heavens. Indeed in one celebrated passage he defies those who say that cool, calm rationality is the mark of the philosopher and the sage. He outlines four types of madness which have divine origins, the last of which is erotic madness; and he asserts that each kind of madness enhances one's understanding of truth.

The erotic feelings to which Socrates refers are homosexual; in particular, they are the love of an older man for a young man, who is also his pupil. The assumption that homosexuality, which borders on paedophilia, is not only acceptable, but also quite normal and desirable, is one way in which the culture of ancient Athens differs from our own. Another is the social and economic structure which allowed large numbers of men to engage in philosophical, and also political, debate. They had slaves who did all the manual work on their behalf; and they had wives who ran their homes and raised their children. A further difference is the smallness of this elite group. Although Athens for centuries was a major cultural and political centre, it was by modern standards very modest in size – little more than a large market town. And the elite was a minority within this community, so that they mostly knew one another personally, or at least by name and reputation.

Yet there are also important ways in which Athens was similar to the modern world. There was remarkable freedom of thought. And although Socrates was eventually accused of traversing the boundaries of that freedom, even in the final days before his death he was debating a wide range of issues, some quite controversial. It was also taken for granted that strength of argument, rather than strength of personality or political power, should win the day. Indeed Socrates was charged with being so clever that he could make weaker arguments win over stronger – a charge he vigorously denied. In ancient Athens, as in the modern world, the values of free thought and debate did not always prevail, but we have in common that these values are highly prized.

The most intriguing similarity is in attitudes to religion. A thousand years after Socrates, when Christianity had established itself as the dominant religion of the Mediterranean world, religion was regarded primarily as a matter of belief. The individual was required to accept a set of dogmas formulated by the Church; and the most grievous sin was that of heresy. To Socrates belief was quite unimportant; religion was a process of spiritual exploration, by which individuals discovered the truth for themselves. In the past century the Socratic approach has again become popular. Only a small minority are now willing to accept doctrinal formulae as the authority of religious institutions. But spiritual exploration, in many and varied forms, is as popular as ever. If Socrates were alive today, and spoke as he did two and a half millennia ago, he would undoubtedly acquire a large and devoted following – and transcriptions of his discourses would sell in huge numbers.

* * *

Socrates was born around the year 470 BC. His father moved in high social circles, and may have been a sculptor. By the age of thirty Socrates was already making his mark among the leading philosophers and scientists of Athens. At this stage his main interest seems to have been geometry and astronomy. And by his early fifties he had become so well-known for his intellectual virtuosity that he was the subject of at least two plays. But he did not confine himself to academic pursuits: he served as an infantryman in two wars, where his physical endurance and calm courage won high praise. He avoided politics because he felt that political office would compel him to compromise his moral principles. Nonetheless on two occasions, at great risk to himself, he protested loudly at political injustices.

His appearance, character and way of life were constant objects of fascination for his contemporaries. He was short and stout, with prominent eyes, a broad, snub nose, and a wide mouth. He enjoyed good food and wine, and had little sympathy with those who abstained from life's pleasures in the name of religion. He also had a keen sense of humour, enjoying the paradoxes of human nature and conduct. Yet he showed no interest in material advancement. On the contrary, in his pursuit of knowledge, and his desire to help others in this pursuit, he ignored his own physical needs and those of his family, enduring great poverty. And the main target of his ironical humour was himself, presenting himself frequently as rather dull and as a slave to passion. He disliked pretentiousness in others, and was rather ruthless with any signs of pretentiousness in himself. As a result he evoked profound love and devotion in his friends, who described him as 'the most moral man of his day'.

Socrates spent little time at home, preferring to spend his time in the streets and market-places of Athens, and especially in the various gymnasia, where he could debate philosophical issues with the other educated people of the city. As the dialogues recorded by his younger contemporary Plato confirm, he was superb at debate and witty in conversation. At one point the oracle at Delphi pronounced that Socrates was the wisest person alive. Socrates was perplexed at this, and made it his mission to test the oracle's utterance. He spoke in turn to all those who claimed or were reputed to be wise, examining them closely to see if they possessed greater wisdom than he did. These examinations became hugely popular, attracting large numbers of spectators. He spoke first to philosophers, then to poets and dramatists, and finally to skilled craftsmen. Among the philosophers he found that those with the highest reputations had the least insight. The poets and dramatists seemed to possess less understanding of their own compositions than their audiences. And while Socrates was impressed by their abilities in their various trades, he found that the craftsmen were ignorant outside their trades. But in Socrates' eyes they all failed in one crucial respect: they believed themselves to have more knowledge than they did. And he concluded that true wisdom consists in an honest approach towards the limitations of one's wisdom.

It is this honesty which makes Socrates' ideas so attractive and stimulating. He does not propose any all-embracing philosophical system, but invites his listeners to join him in an inner pilgrimage. And while he holds the process of rational thought in the highest respect, he does not regard it as the only means of discerning truth. In a celebrated passage in *Phaedrus* he praises madness as the channel of great blessings; and he believes truth is attained by combining rationality with particular forms of madness. The form which interests him most is that of falling in love with another person. This is because the beauty perceived in the object of love is a sign of perfect divine beauty. Thus erotic madness can become the soul's first steps on a path that leads upwards to God.

Behind this attitude towards sexual beauty lay Socrates' most distinct philosophical idea, the so-called doctrine of forms. This states that every human term, such as 'good' or 'beautiful' which denotes some particular, distinct quality, refers to its perfect form; and thus perfect form can only be apprehended by pure thought. So the qualities which our senses perceive are only secondary, deriving from forms which are beyond the senses. This raises the question of how the individual can attain pure thought. To Socrates this is the particular vocation of the philosopher; and it involves gradually detaching the soul from all kinds of bodily sensations, so that it is free from all external disturbance. Philosophy is thus not just an intellectual pursuit, but a way of life in which pleasure and pain, wealth and poverty, respect and contempt, become matters of indifference.

Socrates attracted love and loathing in equal measure. His mission to test the wisdom of others naturally made him unpopular among those whose lack of wisdom he exposed. And his high-minded protests against political injustice provoked the dislike of those who perpetrated injustice in the pursuit of power. His enemies had their revenge in 399 BC when they brought charges against him, and he was forced to stand trial. He was accused of 'corrupting the young', by which was meant turning them against the State; and also of 'neglecting the gods whom the city worships'. Socrates treated the charges with contempt, using the trial as a forum for explaining and justifying his way of life. He was found guilty, and his prosecutors asked for the penalty of death. Socrates had the right to suggest an alternative; and probably the court would have accepted a smaller punishment, such as exile. But Socrates asserted that he really deserved to be treated like a public benefactor, receiving a pension from the State. This incensed the court, and the death penalty was passed.

Normally a condemned man was required to drink hemlock within twenty-four hours. But the trial of Socrates ended during a religious season when judicial deaths were not permitted. So Socrates remained in prison for a month, receiving friends daily and conversing with them in his usual manner. Plato's records of these conversations contain some of Socrates' most profound and moving discourses. His companion Crito suggests that Socrates should try to escape. This prompts Socrates to speak about the relationship of the individual and the State. He argues that individuals are creatures of the State, in that their birth, upbringing and education all take place in the context of laws and customs sanctioned by the state. Thus individuals have a duty to submit to the decrees and verdicts of the State, even when they appear unjust.

To a large group of friends Socrates speaks of his

calm joy at the prospect of death. Throughout his life he had believed in the immortality of the soul, and had spoken eloquently about it. Now he speaks of the philosopher's life as a long preparation for death. In his quest for knowledge the philosopher must gradually separate the soul from the body, making the soul indifferent to the pleasures and pains which the body experiences; in this way the soul comes to apprehend spiritual truth directly. Thus for the philosopher death is the culmination of his profession, in which the soul is set totally free from the body. Later Socrates speculates at great length about what happens to souls beyond death, incorporating many older mythical ideas about the earth and the underworld into his scheme. He acknowledges that many of the specific details may be incorrect. But the important point is that the fate of the soul depends on the moral and spiritual quality of their existence before death – and the way of life of the philosopher has the happiest outcome.

Plato's account of the death of Socrates is simultaneously intensely moving and profoundly peaceful. Socrates himself is almost playful as the moment of death approaches, teasing Crito for his anxieties about the burial arrangements. Socrates then has a bath, and bids farewell to his family. The prison officer, whose duty is to supervise the death, has become so devoted to Socrates that he cannot bear to stay. The poison is then brought in; and after a short prayer Socrates drinks it. His friends, who until now have restrained their emotions, burst into tears. Socrates rebukes them, and they manage to control themselves. Gradually the hemlock takes effect, and the great philosopher quietly slips away.

* * *

Socrates would certainly have preferred his name to have been forgotten after his death; he despised those who hankered after fame. And since he himself wrote nothing, that would have been his most likely fate. But two men who knew him during the last decade of his life, Xenophon and Plato, recorded many of his conversations and speeches. Xenophon's work has usually been regarded with some suspicion: his relations with Socrates were not close and, besides, he seems to have derived much of his material from Plato. So in the present book only Plato's records are used. It has always been suspected that to some degree Plato used Socrates as a mouth-piece for his own ideas; and certainly it is hard to believe that Plato gives us a precise transcription of Socrates' words. Moreover, in the first piece contained in this book, Socrates himself uses the technique of putting his thoughts in the mouth of another person – in this case a wise prophetess. Nonetheless the consensus among scholars is that Plato is largely faithful.

The words of Socrates, as recorded by Plato, are

entirely embedded in dialogues of one kind or another, in which Socrates is addressing himself to one or more people, and responding to their points and questions. Sometimes the conversations are snappy, with each person making short, sharp points; and sometimes the participants, especially Socrates, hold forth at greater length. This has the advantage of presenting ideas in a dramatic fashion. But it is often not easy to pick out the main themes, and to follow the line of Socrates' thought. In this book Socrates' words are presented on their own; and they are divided into chapters according to both source and theme. The chapter headings indicate the sources, so readers who wish to explore the dramatic contexts can easily turn to one of the many English translations of Plato's works.

ROBERT VAN DE WEYER

THE PHILOSOPHY OF LOVE

from *The Symposium* 202a–202c

I will try to give you the philosophy of love which I once heard from a woman in Mantinea, called Diotema. This woman had great spiritual power: on one occasion, when the people of Athens had been unsuccessfully offering sacrifices to avert a plague, she managed to avert the plague for ten years. But now I want to concentrate on her instructions in the art of love; and I will give the best account I can of what she told me....

'Is Love ugly and bad?' I asked her. 'Do not say such things,' she answered; 'do you think that, merely because something is not beautiful, it is necessarily ugly?' 'Of course I do.' 'And that, because something is not wisdom, it is ignorance? Do you not know that there is a state of mind half-way between wisdom and ignorance?' 'What do you mean?' 'I mean,' she replied, 'holding true beliefs without being able to give reasons for them. Surely you see that such a state of mind cannot be called wisdom, because nothing irrational deserves that name. But it would be equally wrong to call it ignorance. How can you call a state of mind ignorance if it possesses truth? Holding true beliefs is a condition half-way between wisdom and ignorance.' 'I accept what you say,' I answered.

'Then do not assert,' said Diotema, 'that what is not beautiful is ugly, and that what is not good is bad. Do not think that, because Love is not good and beautiful, he must for that reason be ugly and bad. Instead you should regard Love as somewhere between the two.' 'And yet,' I said, 'everyone looks upon Love as a great god.' 'When you say everyone,' she responded, 'do you mean those who do not know Love, or are you including those who do?' 'I mean absolutely everybody,' I said. She burst out laughing, and said: 'Well, Socrates, I do not see how Love can be called a great god by those who do not regard Love as divine at all.' 'Who are they?' I asked. 'You are one of them, and I am another.' 'What do you mean?' 'It is perfectly clear. You would say surely that all gods are happy and beautiful. You would not dare to suggest that any of the gods is not.' 'Certainly not.' 'And would you agree that happiness implies the secure enjoyment of what is good and beautiful?' 'Certainly.' 'Yet you have agreed that because Love lacks what is good and beautiful, it desires them.' 'Yes, I have.' 'But that which lacks goodness and beauty cannot be a god.' 'Obviously not.' 'So you see that you are one of those people who believe that love is not a god.'

So I asked Diotema: 'What can Love be, if he is

not a god? A mortal?' 'Far from it,' she answered. 'Then what?' 'As in my previous examples, Love is half-way between two things; he is half-way between being mortal and immortal.' 'What sort of being is that, Diotema?' 'Love is a great spirit, Socrates. Everything that is a spirit is half-god and half-man.' 'And what is the function of such a being?' 'To convey and interpret messages to the gods from humans, and to humans from the gods. From humans Love carries prayers and sacrifices to the gods. From the gods Love carries commands and rewards to humans. Being half-god and half-human, Love is a spiritual bridge between divinity and humanity; he thus prevents the universe from splitting into two separate halves. Across this bridge comes all divine wisdom and all supernatural skills.... God does not deal directly with human beings. It is through the intermediate spirit of Love that intercourse and communication take place between gods and human beings – both when human beings are awake and when they are asleep. Those who possess supernatural insight and skills are therefore spiritual people; while those whose skills are confined to handicraft are earthly creatures....'

'Who are the parents of Love?' I asked. 'That is rather a long story,' Diotema answered, 'but I will tell you. On the day that Aphrodite was born the gods were having a feast. Among them was Contrivance, the son of Invention. After the meal was over Poverty passed by; and seeing that a party was in progress she came to the door and begged. Contrivance was drunk with nectar – wine, I should add, had not yet been discovered – and went out into Zeus' garden, where he was overcome with sleep. So Poverty, thinking that she could alleviate her wretched condition by bearing Contrivance's child, lay down with him and conceived Love. Since Love was conceived on Aphrodite's birthday, and since he has innate passion for all that is beautiful – and since Aphrodite is so beautiful – Love became the servant and follower of Aphrodite.

'Having Contrivance for his father and Poverty for his mother, Love has the following character. He is always poor. Thus, far from being sensitive and beautiful as most people imagine, Love is hard and weather-beaten. He has no shoes for his feet, and no house to live in; he has to sleep outside on the ground, on doorsteps or in the street. Like his mother, he is constantly in want. But, being his father's son, he is constantly scheming to get what he wants; and, above all, he wants whatever is beautiful and good. He is bold, impetuous and energetic; he is always devising tricks like a cunning huntsman; and he is full of ideas. He yearns after knowledge and is devoted to wisdom; he is a skilful magician, an alchemist and a sophist. He is neither mortal nor immortal: within the same day he will live and flourish as things go well, and also meet his death; then he will come to life again with the vigour he inherits from his father. What he wins he always loses. He is neither rich nor poor, neither wise nor ignorant.'

Diotema continued: 'The truth of the matter is this. No god is a lover of knowledge or desires to be wise, because gods are wise already. The same applies to wise human beings, if any exist. Equally those who are ignorant do not love knowledge or desire wisdom. Indeed, the tiresome thing about ignorance is that those who lack beauty, goodness and intelligence are perfectly satisfied with themselves – they do not know what they lack, so they cannot desire them.'

'If neither the wise nor the ignorant desires wisdom,' I asked, 'who does desire wisdom?' Diotema replied: 'A child could answer that question. Obviously those who desire wisdom are in an intermediate class; and this includes Love. Wisdom is one of the most beautiful things which exists; and since Love loves beauty, it follows that Love must desire wisdom. This means that Love is in a state half-way between wisdom and ignorance. This comes from the circumstances of his birth: his father was wise with a fertile mind, while his mother was impractical and helpless. So much for the status of Love, my dear Socrates. As for what you thought about the nature of

Love, your error is quite common. You seem to identify Love with the object of Love, rather than with the subject who feels Love; that is why you believed that Love is supremely beautiful. The object of Love is indeed exquisitely beautiful, and a perfect source of joy; but, as I have just described, the subject which feels Love has a quite different character.'

'Your words carry conviction, Diotema,' I said; 'so tell me, in the light of what you say about the nature of Love, what is the function of Love in human beings?' 'Socrates,' she replied, 'that is precisely what I shall try to teach you. I have already described to you the nature and the parentage of Love; and you have said that Love is devoted to beauty. But suppose someone asked us to explain more precisely this Love of beauty; in particular if we were asked the purpose of this Love which is felt by the lover of beauty.' 'His purpose is to gain possession of beautiful things,' I answered. 'But that merely raises a further question. What will be gained by the person who possesses beautiful things?' I said that I had no immediate answer to this question. 'Well,' Diotema said, 'let us change our terms, substituting good for beautiful. Then suppose someone asks you the purpose of Love which is felt by the lover of the good.' 'Possession of the good,' I replied. 'And what will be gained by the person who possesses the good?' 'I find that an easier question to answer: he will be happy.' 'This is pre-

sumably,' replied Diotema, 'because happiness consists in the possession of the goods. Once one has
given that answer, the inquiry is at an end; there is no
need to ask the further question, as to why a person
desires to be happy.' 'Quite so.'

'Now, do you suppose,' asked Diotema, 'that all
people desire and love the good, and that all people
constantly wish to possess the good?' 'Yes,' replied
Socrates, 'I believe that all people are the same in this
regard.' 'If that is so, Socrates, why do we not speak
of all people being in love, but rather say that some
are in love, while others are not?' 'I wonder what the
reason can be,' I replied. 'There is no need to wonder,' Diotema continued; 'the truth is that we isolate
a particular kind of love, giving it the name of Love.
But the name of Love really belongs to Love as a
whole, and we should use different names for each
kind of Love.' 'Can you give me an example of
another word used in this way?' 'Yes, here is one. In
its original usage, poetry simply means creation; and
creation, as you know, can take many forms. Any
action which causes a thing to emerge from non-exis-
tence into existence may be called poetry. Thus all the
various crafts are forms of poetry, and all craftsmen
should be called poets.' 'Yes.' 'But in fact they are not
called poets, but are called by other names. Out of the
whole sphere of poetry or creation only one part,
which deals with music and metre, is isolated and

called by the name of the whole. This part alone is called poetry, and those whose field is this kind of poetry are called poets.' 'Quite true.'

'It is just the same with Love,' continued Diotema. 'The general term embraces every desire for good and for happiness; that indicates how almighty and all-embracing Love is. But this desire expresses itself in many ways. Those who love money, or physical prowess, or wisdom, are not said to be in love, and so they are not called lovers. But those whose passion runs in one particular channel usurp the name of lover, which should belong to everyone; they alone are said to be lovers and in love.' 'There seems to be truth in what you say,' I remarked. 'Indeed,' Diotema continued, 'there is a theory that lovers are people in search of the other half of themselves. But in my view, dear friend, love is not desire for either the half or the whole – unless the half or the whole happens to be good. People are quite willing to have their feet or their hands amputated if they believe those parts of themselves to be diseased. The truth is, I think, that people are not attached to what particularly belongs to them; they are attached to what they regard as good, regardless of whether they own it or not. The only object of Love is what is good. Do you not agree?' 'I certainly do agree,' I replied. 'May we then say without qualification that people are in love with what is good?' 'Yes.' 'And not only its possession, but its perpetual possession?' 'Certainly.' 'To sum up, then, Love is the desire for the perpetual possession of the good.' 'That is most certainly true.'

'Now that we have established the invariable nature of Love,' Diotema continued, 'we must ask in what way, and by what sort of behaviour, people must express this intense desire, if it is to deserve the name Love. What sort of function will this desire have? Can you tell me?' 'If I could, Diotema, I should not be feeling such admiration for your wisdom, or asking you to be my teacher in these matters.' 'Well,' she said, 'I will tell you. The function is to procreate what is beautiful, and this procreation can be either physical or spiritual.' 'What you are saying needs an interpreter; I don't understand.' 'I will put it more clearly. All people, Socrates, have an impulse to procreate; and this impulse is both spiritual and physical. When they reach maturity, they feel a natural desire to have children; and the process of bringing children to birth is always beautiful, never ugly. Indeed, this process is divine: conceiving and bringing a child to birth is a sacred activity, in which there can be no disharmony. Ugliness is out of harmony with the divine, whereas beauty is in harmony. Thus Beauty is the goddess who presides over birth; and when people in a state of desire come into contact with beauty, they experience that serenity and carefree joy that makes procreation possible. But when ugliness is near, this effect is just the opposite: they become sullen, and withdraw into themselves, suppressing the feelings of desire that stir within them. So those in whom desire is already strong are passionately attracted towards beauty, because beauty can satisfy the desire and relieve the tension it causes.'

Diotema continued: 'You should not conclude from this, Socrates, that the object of Love is beauty.' 'What is his object, then?' 'His object is to procreate; beauty is the means whereby this object is attained.' 'Is that so?' 'I assure you it is. So why is procreation the object of Love? Because procreation is the closest a human being can get to immortality. If, as we agreed, the purpose of Love is the perpetual possession of the good, it follows that Love must desire immortality together with the good. And thus we must recognise that Love has twin objects: immortality and the good.'

All this, then, I learnt from Diotema on the several occasions when she spoke to me on the subject of love. One day she asked me: 'What do you suppose, Socrates, is the cause of this love and this desire? Look at the behaviour of other creatures, animals and birds. Whenever the desire to procreate comes over them, they are seized by violent feelings of love. Their first aim is to achieve sexual union, and the second is to provide food and shelter for their young. To achieve these aims they are ready to fight with all their strength, and even to die; they are ready to starve and to make any other sacrifice to ensure the survival of their progeny. With human beings you might suppose that such behaviour was the result of rational thought. But what is the cause of this intense love among animals? Can you tell me?' I confessed that I had no idea. 'How can you expect to become an expert on the subject of love, if you cannot begin to answer this question?' 'As I have said before, Diotema, my ignorance is the reason why I have come to you. I know that I need a teacher. So tell me the cause of this, and of all the other phenomena connected with love.'

'Well,' answered Diotema, 'if you believe that the natural object is what we have already agreed, on more than one occasion, the answer will not surprise you. The same argument applies to animals as to humans. Mortal flesh seeks, as far as possible, to perpetuate itself and become immortal. The only way in which it can achieve this is by procreation, which ensures the continuing replacement of old members of its species with new. Even over the span in which particular individuals live and retain their identities – a man is called by the same name from boyhood to old age – they do not in fact retain the same attributes; they are continuously being renewed, undergoing a constant process of loss and reparation, which affects the hair, the skin, the bones, the blood and the whole body. The soul too is involved in this process. No person's character, habits, opinions, desires, pleasures, pains and fears remain always the same; new ones appear and old ones disappear. Thus our knowledge is just as much open to change as the other attributes I have mentioned; each piece of knowledge is as subject to a degree of change as the person as a whole. When we speak of recollection, we imply that knowledge departs from us; forgetting is the departure of knowledge, and recollection, by implanting a fresh mental image in place of the one that has been lost, preserves it, giving the spurious appearance that no loss occurred. This is the way in which everything mortal is preserved. Only divinity can remain forever the same; mortal beings are preserved by a process in which the losses caused by age are repaired by new acquisitions of a similar kind. This device, Socrates, enables mortals to partake of immortality, both physically and spiritually – although truly immortal beings enjoy immortality in a different manner. So do not feel surprised that every creature naturally cherishes its own progeny; it is in order to attain immortality that all are gripped by this desire and love.'

I was astonished at what she said, and I responded: 'You may be very wise, Diotema, but am I really to believe this?' 'Certainly you are,' she answered, with the assurance of her profession. 'If you will reflect further, you will see that human ambition provides an example of the same truth. You will be astonished at the irrationality of human ambition unless you bear in mind what I have said. Love of fame, and the desire to achieve something whose glory will never die, are extremely powerful emotions. For this fame and glory, even more than for their children, people are ready to run risks, spend their wealth, endure every kind of hardship, and even lay down their lives…. The desire for lasting renown and high reputation is the incentive for numerous actions; and the stronger people are, the greater is the incentive. People are in love with immortality. Those whose creative instinct is physical express this love through sexual activity, believing that through their children they can secure for themselves a degree of immortality, and be remembered for long into the future. But there are some whose creative instinct is within the soul, and who thus long to have spiritual progeny. And if you ask what spiritual progeny a soul can have, the answer is wisdom and virtue….'

'So far,' continued Diotema, 'I have dealt with the mysteries of love in which even you could probably be initiated – although whether you could understand the revelation to which they lead the true seeker, I do not know. However, you shall not fail to understand this revelation for any lack of effort on my part. I will tell you of it; and I ask you to respond if you can.

'A man who wishes to follow the right way to this goal must begin, when he is young, by learning to contemplate physical beauty. If he is properly directed by a wise guide, he will first fall in love with one particular beautiful person, and share fine feelings of affection. Later he will observe that physical beauty in one person is closely akin to physical beauty in any other; and, if he is to make outward physical beauty the object of his quest, he would be foolish not to acknowledge that the beauty exhibited in all bodies is in truth the same. When he has reached this conclusion, he will become a lover of all physical beauty. He will grow less intense in his passion for one particular person, realising that such a passion is low and trivial.

'The next stage,' Diotema continued, 'is for the man to regard beauty of soul as more valuable than beauty of body. The result will be that, when he encounters a virtuous soul in a body which has little physical beauty, he will be happy to love and cherish that person; and he himself will be uplifted by this love. This in turn will compel him to contemplate beauty as it exists in various human activities and institutions; and he will recognise that here too all beauty is akin. He will be thus led to regard all kinds of physical beauty as greatly inferior to spiritual beauty. From here he should be directed to the sciences, contemplating their beauty also. Then he will be able to perceive beauty in its widest sense. He will no longer be the slave of a base and narrow devotion to a particular example of beauty – be it a person or an activity – but he will be able to scan the entire ocean of beauty. This love of beauty in its entirety will bring forth many noble sentiments and wise ideas until at last, strengthened and enhanced in stature by this experience, he catches sight of one unique science – of which I will now speak. The object of this science is a special kind of beauty.

'I must ask you,' Diotema said, 'to pay the closest attention to what I am about to say. Those who have been guided to this point in the mysteries of love, and who have directed their thoughts towards examples of beauty in the proper order, will have completed their initiation. Then suddenly a beauty will be revealed to them which is utterly wonderful, and which, Socrates, is the final goal of all their previous efforts. This beauty is eternal: it neither comes into being nor passes away; it neither waxes nor wanes. It is not partly beautiful and partly ugly, nor beautiful from one aspect and ugly from another, nor beautiful to some and ugly to others. It is quite different from the beauty of a face or hands or anything physical; nor is it like the beauty of a philosophy or a science; nor is it like the beauty which derives from being part of something bigger than itself, like the beauty of a natural scene. They will see that this beauty is absolute; it is complete within itself; it is unique and eternal. It is the beauty from which all other beautiful things derive their beauty; yet, while other things come into being and pass away, this beauty cannot be enhanced or diminished, or undergo any kind of change.

'People can only perceive this beauty,' continued Diotema, 'when they have developed and refined their feelings of love for others to a very high degree. Indeed, this is the right way to be initiated into the mysteries of love. People must begin with examples of physical beauty, and ascend step by step to the absolute beauty which is their goal. They should learn to appreciate one example of physical beauty; progress from one example to two, and from two to all; then move upwards from physical beauty to moral beauty, and from moral beauty to the beauty of knowledge, and from particular kinds of knowledge to the supreme knowledge whose sole object is absolute beauty. Only by working steadily upwards in this way is it possible to know absolute beauty.

'My dear Socrates,' the woman from Mantinea went on, 'this is the place where a person's life should be spent – the spiritual place where absolute beauty is contemplated. Once you have seen absolute beauty, you will not value it in terms of gold or fine clothing or sexual activity. At present all these things enthral you. You, and many like you, go into such ecstasy that, provided you could always enjoy them, you would even go without food and drink to have them. But when people perceive absolute beauty in its pure and divine essence, existing apart and alone, they have no taste for these tainted, physical forms of beauty. Do you regard the lives of those whose gaze is fixed in the direction of absolute beauty, who can contemplate absolute beauty and are in union with it, as in some way impoverished? Do you not see that in this place alone, in the spiritual place where absolute beauty can be seen, it is possible to discern true goodness – not mere reflected images of goodness, but true goodness itself. And those who have successfully nurtured this capacity to perceive absolute beauty will have the privilege of being loved by God; they will become, as far as it is possible for humans, immortal.'

This is what Diotema said to me, and this is what I believe. And since I believe it, I try to persuade others that the best helper in the attainment of happiness is Love. I declare that it is the duty of all people to honour Love. I now honour and practise the mysteries of Love to a high degree, and I recommend others to do the same. I praise the power and valour of Love to the best of my ability; and I will always do so. I have now finished what I have to say. If you wish, you can call it a panegyric, delivered in honour of Love; otherwise you can give it whatever name you please.

THE IMMORTALITY OF THE SOUL

from *Phaedrus* (245–248)

Every soul is immortal, because that which is always in motion is immortal. But that which owes its motion to something else, even though it may cause motion in other things, is mortal because its motion may cease. Only that which moves itself is immortal, since it could not cease to be in motion without being false to its own nature; it is the source and prime origin of motion in all other things that move. A prime origin cannot come into being. All that comes into being must derive its existence from a prime origin, but the prime origin itself must come from nothing; for if a prime origin were derived from anything, it would no longer be a prime origin.... Thus we prove that what moves is immortal; and people should feel no hesitation in recognising the soul, in both its essence and its definition as immortal. If a body had its source of motion outside itself, it would be soulless; but a body which moves itself from within must be endowed with a soul, since self-motion is of the essence of soul. And since we have established that what moves itself is identical with soul, it inevitably follows that soul is uncreated and immortal.

Now we must try to give an account of the soul's immortality. To describe this immortality precisely would require an exposition of such length and depth that only a god could deliver it; but human beings are able to say more briefly what the soul resembles. Let us use an image, and compare the soul with a winged charioteer and his team of horses, acting together. The horses belonging to the gods are good and come from good stock; but those belonging to humans are a mixture of good and bad. Each human being is required to drive a pair of horses; and while one of these horses is fine, from good and noble stock, the other is opposite in every way. So for humans the task of the charioteer is necessarily difficult and unpleasant.

Now we must explore in more depth how it is that human beings are both mortal and immortal – they consist of both body and soul. Taken together souls are in charge of all that is inanimate, and permeates the entire universe, appearing at different times in different forms. When it is perfect and has wings, the soul flies freely and governs all creation; but the soul that has lost its wings falls until it encounters solid matter. There it settles, and puts on an earthly body. The power of the soul makes the body appear to be self-moving; and this combination of body and soul is what we call life, and we term it as mortal.

So let us now consider why a soul may fly or fail to fly. The reason is something like this. The function of a wing is to take what is heavy, and raise it upwards to the region where the gods dwell. Of all things connected with the body, the soul has the greatest affinity with the divine, which is endowed with beauty, wisdom, goodness and every other attribute of excellence. These attributes are the prime source of nourishment and growth to the wings of the soul; but their opposites, such as ugliness and evil, cause the wings to waste and perish.... Those souls with fine wings, whose chariots are pulled by horses that are well-matched and tractable, fly easily across the vault of heaven. But others, with vicious horses which have not been broken in, are dragged down in the direction of the earth; and they are thus caught in a terrible and agonising struggle.

Souls that are termed immortal, as they reach the summit of heaven, go outside the vault and stand on the back of the universe. And as they stand there, they are carried round by its revolutions, which enables them to contemplate what lies outside the heavens. No mortal poet has ever sung, or ever will sing, verses that describe this region as it deserves. Nevertheless we must have the courage to speak the truth, especially as truth itself is our theme. The region of which I speak is where reality dwells; it is the object of true knowledge. It is without colour or shape, and cannot be touched; yet it is utterly real, and can be apprehended only by the intellect, which is the pilot of the soul. So the minds of gods and immortal souls, sustained by pure intelligence and knowledge, are satisfied with this vision of reality; and they are nourished and made happy by the contemplation of truth, until the circular revolution brings them back to their starting-point. In the course of their journey they see absolute justice, discipline and knowledge – not knowledge about things which come into being, not knowledge which varies with the objects we now call real, but the absolute knowledge concerning what is absolutely real in the fullest sense. And when they have in this manner seen and had their fill of the other objects which comprise absolute reality, they withdraw again within the vault of heaven and return home....

Such is the life of the gods. And such too is the life of the other souls which are most similar to gods, and hence able to steer their chariots above the vault of heaven – although the unruly behaviour of their horses impairs their vision of reality. A second class of souls sometimes rises upwards and sometimes sinks, owing to the restiveness of their horses; they see part of reality, not the whole. All the other souls, in spite of their common urge to reach the upper world, fail to do so, and remain below, trampling and jostling one another, each eager to outstrip the others. The struggle and confusion are so great that the wings of many of the souls are broken, and the souls are made lame. So, for all their effort, they fall downwards without ever having glimpsed the vision; and henceforth they can only learn about reality from the reports of others....

Sometimes a soul which has seen something of reality becomes forgetful, or its vision becomes distorted. As a result it loses its wings and falls to earth. Such a soul never takes on the flesh of an animal. Rather it enters a human infant, who is destined to become a seeker after truth, a lover of beauty, or a follower of the Muses ..... In these roles the soul recollects the things which it once perceived when it journeyed with the gods. Then the soul looks downwards from above onto reality; now it looks upwards from below at reality. If these roles are performed well, the soul may regain its wings. And it can do this by recovering as best it can its memories of the divine vision. Through this recollection, which may be called mysticism, human beings can become perfect in the full sense of the word. Such people have no interest in the common objects of human ambition, applying themselves wholly to divine reality. For this reason they are regarded by most people as mad.

IN PRAISE OF MADNESS

from *Phaedrus* (244–245, 249–250)

There are some who argue that, since madness is irrational, it is therefore evil. But in fact madness, provided it comes as a gift of heaven, is the channel by which we receive the greatest blessings. Take, for example, the prophetess at Delphi and the priestesses at Dodona, and consider all the benefits which individuals and communities in Greece have received from them. These benefits are conferred only when they are in a state of frenzy, not when they are sober. And if we are to include the prophetess Sybil and others like her, who by divine inspiration have set many enquirers on the right path forwards, we would be relating at tedious length what people already know. But this at least is worth pointing out: that when our forefathers gave this art of prophecy, the noblest of all arts, a name, they saw no disgrace or fault in madness. Thus they called it the manic art.... They recognised that madness is greater than sobriety, since madness can come from God whereas sobriety is human.

There is a second type of madness which occurs when past sins severely disturb the mind, causing great suffering. This madness appears in the members of certain families, and it can induce its victims to seek relief through prayer and worship. It has frequently been found that religious rituals help to make the victims well, and keep them well. Thus religion is the right cure for this kind of madness, enabling those who suffer from it to have a means of overcoming the effects of past sins.

A third type of madness is possession by the Muses. When this madness grips a gentle and innocent soul, it rouses the soul, inspiring it to compose lyrics and other forms of poetry. In this way the countless deeds of our ancient heroes are glorified, for the instruction of future generations. But if people come to the door of poetry untouched by the madness of the Muses, believing that technique alone will make them good poets, they will not succeed. Some compositions can never attain perfection, and are utterly eclipsed by the performances of inspired madmen.

There is a fourth type of madness which befalls people when they are reminded by the sight of beauty on earth of the true beauty of heaven. They grow spiritual wings and try to fly upwards. But they expose themselves to the charge of insanity because like birds they fix their gaze on the heights above, while neglecting things below. But our discourse points to this, by its nature and its origin, being the best of all forms of divine possession, both for the subjects themselves and for those whose beauty stimulated the upward movement. And it is when someone is touched by this kind of madness – when love is aroused by the beauty of another – that person is called a lover.

THE DEFINITION OF LOVE

from *Phaedrus* (237–238)

In every discussion there is only one way to begin, if one is to reach a sound conclusion: that is to know precisely what one is discussing. Otherwise one is liable to miss the mark entirely. Most people in discussion are quite unaware of their ignorance of the essential nature of their subject, whatever that subject may be. Believing that they know it, they do not begin their discussion by agreeing on the use of terms; and as a result they are soon lost in contradictions and misunderstandings. So let us begin our discussion on the state of being in love by defining the nature and power of love.

As everyone would agree, love is a kind of desire. Yet we know that a person does not have to be in love in order to desire what is beautiful. How then are we to distinguish the state of being a lover from that of not being a lover?

We must realise that in each one of us there are two powerful and dominant principles guiding our actions: the first is the desire for pleasure, which is innate; the second is the determination to attain excellence, which is acquired. These two principles are sometimes in agreement within us and sometimes at odds; at one moment the first principle prevails, at another moment the second. The determination which impels us towards excellence is rational; and the force by which it masters us we call self-control. The desire which pulls us towards pleasure is irrational; and when it masters us, we call it excess. There are many types and forms of excess, and it goes by a variety of names. Those who are ruled by each form of excess are then referred to by its name – a position which should neither be honoured nor valued. If, for example, a person is ruled by the desire for food, a condition which we call gluttony, then that person is called a glutton. If a person is ruled by the desire for drink, a desire which dominates every thought and action, then we know the name by which that person is called. It is the same with all the different sorts of desire and their names: whichever desire happens to prevail, the person subject to that desire is referred to by its name.

The conclusion to which all this is leading is obvious, but for the sake of clarity it should be made explicit. There is a particular irrational desire whose object is beauty; and this desire is powerfully reinforced by bodily instincts. The name of this desire is passionate love. And when the desire prevails over the rational determination to attain excellence and emerges victorious, the person subject to it is called a lover.

THE CONDITION OF LOVE

―――――◆―――――

from *Phaedrus* (250–253)

Beauty shines brightly in the world above the vault of heavens; and here below it also shines very clearly. And the sense by which we apprehend beauty is the keenest of all our senses, although it does not bring knowledge. Indeed, if we could perceive knowledge and other spiritual entities with our eyes, the love aroused within us would be overpowering. But as it is, beauty is the greatest quality and the most lovely which our eyes can see. Those who have no sense of the region above the heavens, or who have been corrupted, cannot easily make the transition from beauty on earth to absolute beauty. So when they see beauty on earth they feel no reverence for it. On the contrary, they surrender themselves to sensuality, becoming eager like animals to mate and have children; or in their addiction to pleasure they feel no fear or shame in pursuing desires which are unnatural.

But those who have seen fully the celestial vision are able to recognise in a beautiful face or physical form the reflection of ideal beauty. First of all they tremble, feeling something of the awe which the celestial vision itself inspired. Next they gaze upon it and worship it as if it were divine; and, if they were not afraid of being thought utterly mad, they would offer sacrifices as they would to the image of a god. Then, as happens after a cold fit, their condition changes, and they break into an unaccustomed sweat. Through their eyes they receive an emanation of beauty, by which the feathers on the soul's wings are nourished. The wings grow hot, and this is accompanied by a softening of the passages from which the feathers grow; these passages had long since become parched and closed, preventing new feathers from shooting. As the nourishing moisture falls upon the soul, the roots of each feather under the surface of the soul swell and push upwards. In this the soul begins to regain its original state, when it was covered with feathers. So now the soul throbs with agitation; in fact the soul whose feathers are beginning to grow has the same irritating sensation of pricking and itching which children feel in their gums when they start to cut their teeth.

When the soul in this condition gazes on the beautiful object of its love, and is nurtured and warmed by the emanation that floods over it – which is why we speak of a 'flood' of longing – all pain disappears, and is replaced by gladness. But when it is separated from the object of its love, it becomes parched, and the passages through which the feathers shoot close up through lack of moisture, obstructing any fresh growth. The embryo feathers yearn to push upwards, but are imprisoned below the surface, where they throb like a pulse against their proper outlets. The soul is driven mad by the pain which pricks across its entire surface. And yet it continues to feel some pleasure in recalling the beauty of its beloved.

The man who experiences this mixture of pleasure and pain is perplexed by its strangeness, and they struggle helplessly. In this frenzy he cannot sleep at night or relax by day. He feels driven to seek out the one whose beauty has driven them to this state. And when he sees the object of their love, the soul is refreshed by the flood of emanations, and the closed passages are opened. He obtains a respite from the pricks of pain, and instead enjoys a momentary sweetness which nothing can equal. From this state he would never willingly emerge. In his eyes nothing can compare with his beloved. Mother, brothers and friends are all forgotten; he would even think nothing of losing all his property. The conventions of civilised behaviour, which he used to observe with pride, he now scorns. He is willing to become slave to his beloved, and to do anything to remain near. Apart from the reverence he feels for the possessor of such beauty, he has found the only physician for the most grievous kind of sickness....

Each soul in its incarnation on earth, so long as it remains uncorrupted, spends its time in worshipping and trying to imitate a particular god. This is the god whose devotee it was prior to falling down to earth. The soul conducts itself on earth towards others and the world in general according to the example of this god. Thus in selecting someone to love from among those who possess beauty, a man follows the inclination of his soul. The beauty of the one he chooses must reflect in some measure the beauty of the god he worships, so he can treat his beloved as divine.... Every man desires to find in his beloved a nature comparable with his own particular divinity. And when his search is successful, he devotes himself to persuading and training his beloved to imitate that god in behaviour and attitude – and he himself tries to imitate that god too. There is no room for jealousy or spite; he concentrates all his efforts to leading his beloved and himself towards perfect imitation of his god. This is the aspiration of the true lover. And the one who captures the affections of a lover – who drives another person mad with love – enjoys glorious happiness.

IN PURSUIT OF WISDOM

———◆———

from *The Apology* (20d–23e)

I am reputed to possess a form of wisdom. What form of wisdom is this? Human wisdom, I presume. This means I am wise only in a very limited sense. There are some geniuses possessing forms of wisdom which are more than human; indeed I do not know how else to account for it, because I certainly do not share the knowledge which they have, and anyone claiming that I do is lying and trying to slander me. Nonetheless I will now make what seems an extravagant claim. Please do not interrupt me, for the tale I will tell is not so much about me, as about an unimpeachable authority, the god at Delphi. I call this god as witness to my wisdom.

I presume that you know Chaerephon … and you know what he was like; how enthusiastic he was over everything that he undertook. One day he actually went to Delphi and asked this question: 'Is anyone wiser than Socrates?' The answer came that there was no one.… When I heard about the oracle's answer, I asked myself: 'What is the god saying, and what is his hidden meaning? I am well aware that I have no claim to wisdom, great or small. So what can the god mean by claiming that I am the wisest man in the world? He cannot be telling a lie; that would not be possible.'

After puzzling over this for some time, I finally decided with great reluctance to check the truth of the god's answer by going to interview a man with a high reputation for wisdom. I felt that here, if anywhere, I could succeed in disproving the oracle, pointing out to the divine authority: 'You said that I am the wisest of men, but here is a man who is wiser.'

I thoroughly examined this man.... I soon learnt that, just as many people regard him as wise, he regards himself as wise. Yet as our conversation progressed, I formed the opposite view. I then began trying to show him that, despite his own high opinion of himself, he was not truly wise. But my efforts were resented both by him and by the many other people present. As I walked away, I reflected: 'I am certainly wiser than this man. In all probability neither of us possesses any knowledge worth mentioning. But the difference is this: he thinks he knows something which he does not know; whereas I am quite aware of my own ignorance. So it seems that in this small way I am wiser than he is: I do not think I know what I do not know.'

After this I went to interview another man with an even greater reputation for wisdom, and I formed the same impression. And here too I incurred the resentment of both the man himself and a number of others.

I proceeded to interview one person after another. I was appalled to find myself becoming quite unpopular, but I felt compelled to put the god's business first. I regarded myself as having a duty to interview everyone with a reputation for knowledge, in order to discover the meaning of the oracle. And I solemnly promise that, as I pursued my investigation at the god's command, my honest impression was this: that the people with the highest reputations were the least wise, while others who were supposed to be inferior possessed far greater insight.

Please think of my adventures as a pilgrimage undertaken to establish the truth of the oracle once and for all. Initially I interviewed men whose fame rested on their philosophical ideas. I then turned to poets of various kinds – dramatic, lyric and the rest – believing that in comparison with them I would be exposed as a complete ignoramus. I would read what I thought were their finest works, and question them closely about the meaning of what they had written, hoping to enlarge my own knowledge. I hesitate to tell the truth, but I feel compelled: it is hardly an exaggeration to say that any of the bystanders could have explained those poems better than the authors themselves. So I soon made up my mind about the poets too: it is not wisdom which enables them to write poetry, but a kind of instinct or inspiration, similar to that found in seers and prophets. We accept that seers and prophets deliver their sublime messages without any idea of their meaning; and it was now clear to me that poets write their verses in the same manner. As I also observed, poets believe that their poetic ability gives them perfect understanding of all other subjects – whereas in truth most poets have little knowledge of anything. So I left that line of inquiry with the same sense of possessing superior wisdom that I had in relation to the philosophers.

Lastly I turned to the skilled craftsmen. I recognised that I had virtually no understanding of their arts, so I was certain that I would be impressed by their knowledge. In this I was not disappointed. They were proficient in matters of which I was ignorant, and in that respect they excelled me in wisdom. But these professional experts seemed to share the same failing which I had noticed in the poets: that on the strength of their technical abilities they claimed perfect insight into all other subjects, even the most important. I felt that this error eclipsed their positive accomplishments. So I became my own oracle, asking myself: 'Is it better to be as I am, neither wise with their wisdom, nor ignorant with their ignorance; or possess both their wisdom and their ignorance?' I replied to myself that it is better to be as I am.

The effect of my investigations has been to arouse against me a great deal of hostility, which has proved especially bitter and persistent; and many malicious remarks have been made. Also many people now apply the term 'wise' to me. This is because, whenever I disproved another person's claim to be knowledgeable about a particular subject, the bystanders assumed that I myself was expert in that subject. But the truth of the matter is that real wisdom belongs to the god; and the oracle is his way of telling us that human wisdom has little or no value. It seems to me the god is not referring literally to me, but is using my name as an example, as if to say to us: 'The wisest among you are those who have realised, like Socrates, that in respect of wisdom they are worthless.'

In obedience to the divine command I still search for people who may possess wisdom. I speak to all people, both citizens of Athens and strangers, who appear to be wise. And when I decide that a person is not wise, I try to assist the god by proving it. This occupation has kept me so busy that I have not had time to engage in politics or look after my own affairs. In fact my service to the god has reduced me to extreme poverty.

A number of young men, with wealthy fathers and plenty of leisure, have freely attached themselves to me, because they enjoy hearing other people questioned. Often they take me as their model, questioning people in the same way. As a result bystanders conclude that these young men must be knowledgeable, whereas in truth they know little or nothing. Their victims then become annoyed; but their anger is directed towards me, not them. They complain that I am an interfering pest, who fills young men's heads with wrong ideas. If you ask them what I do or teach that has this effect, they are lost for words, not knowing how to answer. But as they do not want to admit their confusion, they fall back on the stock charges made against any seeker after wisdom: that I teach my pupils about things above the heavens and below the earth, causing them to disbelieve in the gods; and that by my cleverness I make weaker arguments defeat stronger ones. They would, I think, be very reluctant to admit the truth: that they have been exposed as claiming to knowledge which they do not possess. They want, I suppose, to protect their own reputations. Unfortunately they are energetic and numerous, and they speak against me with great vigour and eloquence; and so for a long time they have monopolised your ears.

THE PHILOSOPHER'S VOCATION

from *The Apology* (29c–34b)

Suppose that you acquit me, paying no attention to Anytus, who said that either I should not have come before this court at all, or, since I have come here, I must be put to death because otherwise I would immediately corrupt your sons with my teaching. Suppose that, to guard against my influence, you said to me: 'On this occasion, Socrates, we shall ignore Anytus and acquit you, but on one condition, that you give up your quest for wisdom and stop philosophising. If we find you continuing in this way, you shall be put to death.' Supposing, as I say, that you should offer to acquit me on these terms, I would reply that I am your very grateful and devoted servant, but I owe a greater allegiance to God than to you. And so long as I breathe and have my wits, I shall never stop the study of philosophy; nor shall I stop speaking to those I meet, and guiding them towards the truth.

Moreover, when I encounter people, I shall say in my usual manner: 'My good friend, you are a resident of Athens, a city which is respected and renowned throughout the world for its wisdom and courage.

Are you not ashamed that you devote yourself to acquiring as much money as possible, and to gaining a high position for yourself, but give no attention to matters of truth and to the perfection of your soul?' And when people dispute my words, protesting that they care greatly about truth and spiritual perfection, I shall not let them go or leave them. No, I will question and examine them, testing their sincerity. If it appears that despite their protests they have made no real spiritual progress, I shall rebuke them for neglecting matters of supreme importance in favour of trivialities.

I shall talk in this way to everyone I meet, young and old, foreigners and fellow-citizens – but especially to you, my fellow-citizens, because you are closer to me in kinship. This, I assure you, is what my god commands. And I believe that my service to my god is the greatest good that has befallen this city, because I spend all my time trying to persuade you, young and old, to make the welfare of your souls your highest concern, rather than the pursuit of pleasure and possessions. I proclaim: 'Wealth does not bring goodness, but goodness brings wealth and every other blessing, both to the individual and to the State.'

If I corrupt the young with this message, then you may infer that the message is harmful. But if people say that my message is different from this, they are talking nonsense. Thus, gentlemen, you can please yourselves whether you listen to Anytus or not, and whether you acquit me or not. But be sure that I am not going to change my behaviour, even if I have to die a hundred deaths....

I will now say something else which may provoke an uproar; but please restrain yourselves. If I am what I claim to be, and if you put me to death, you will harm yourselves far more than you harm me. Indeed, neither Meletus nor Anytus can do me any harm at all, because they do not have the power; God's law, as I understand it, does not permit a better man to be harmed by a worse one. No doubt my accuser wants to put me to death, or to have me banished, or to deprive me of civic rights. But if he thinks – in common with many other people, I dare say – that these are great calamities, I do not agree. I believe that he is bringing a far greater calamity on himself, by trying to put a man to death unjustly. For this reason, gentlemen, I am not pleading on my own behalf, as might be supposed; I am actually pleading on yours, to save you from misusing gifts of God by condemning me. If you put me to death, you will not easily find someone to replace me. I will be blunt with you, using a comical image: by divine will I have been assigned to this city, as if to a large thoroughbred horse which, owing to its huge size, is inclined to be lazy, and needs to be stimulated by the stings of a fly.

It seems that I have a divine duty to perform the same service to this city as the fly to the horse. Throughout the day I settle in different places – here, there, and everywhere – rousing you, guiding you, and rebuking you. You will not readily find another man similar to me; so I advise you to spare my life. Yet perhaps you will soon stir from your mental slumber, and in a fit of irritation you will take Anytus' advice, swatting me with a single slap. Then you will be able to continue sleeping till the end of your days – unless God in his love sends someone else to take my place.

If you doubt whether I am really the sort of person to have been sent to this city by God's will, you can persuade yourselves by asking these questions. Does it seem normal that I should have neglected my affairs and ignored the needs of my family, enduring great humiliation, in order to devote myself to your spiritual welfare? Would any human, without divine prompting, become like a father or an elder brother to each one of you, visiting you privately and urging you to think more about goodness? If I had derived any enjoyment from it, or had been paid for my wise advice, then my conduct could have been explained. But you can see for yourselves that, while my accusers shamelessly charge me with all sorts of other crimes, they do not have the impertinence to pretend that I have demanded or requested a fee from anyone. I can offer a witness to prove the truth of my statement: my poverty.

It may seem odd that I should go round giving advice in this way, concerning myself with other people's well-being, and yet I never seek to speak to you as a whole, advising you on affairs of State. I have already indicated a number of times the reason for this, that I am subject to divine, supernatural guidance.... This guidance began in my early childhood, and it is a sort of voice which comes to me. When the voice speaks, it always dissuades me from doing what I propose to do; it never urges me on. It is this voice that prevents me from entering public life. On reflection I can see the wisdom in this: you can be sure that, if I had tried in the past to engage in politics, I would long ago have lost my life, with no benefit either to you or to myself. Please do not take offence if I tell you the truth. No man on earth who, as a matter of conscience, opposes you or any other organised democracy, striving to prevent the State from doing wrong and breaking its own laws, can possibly escape with his life. The true champion of justice, if he intends to survive even for a short time, must confine himself to private matters, and avoid politics entirely.

Do you suppose that I would have lived as long as this if I had engaged in public life, conducting myself in that sphere with integrity? Do you suppose I would have survived if I had upheld the cause of justice, and in obedience to my conscience set justice above all other concerns? Certainly not, gentlemen; nor would any other man. Throughout my life I have been consistent in the performance of both my public and my private duties. I have never approved any action by any person that was incompatible with justice; and at times this has brought me into opposition with some who maliciously call themselves my pupils. I have set myself up as a teacher. But if people, young or old, are eager to hear my conversations in which I fulfil my mission, I never begrudge them the opportunity. I am ready to answer questions from rich and poor alike; and I am ready to speak to others, and then ask them questions. Whether people who hear me become good or bad citizens is not my responsibility, since I have never promised or undertaken to teach anyone anything. And if people assert that they have learned or heard from me in private something not open to others, you may be sure they are not telling the truth.

Why, then, do some people enjoy spending a great deal of time in my company? You have already heard the reason, gentlemen; I have told you quite frankly. It is because they enjoy hearing me examine those who think that they are wise, but who in fact are not. I recognise that part of their pleasure is idle amusement. Nonetheless, as I have said, I have accepted this task in obedience to God's command, given in oracles, dreams and every other way that the gods communicate with human beings. This is a true assertion, which can easily be verified.

I am accused of corrupting some of the young people who hang around me, and of having effectively corrupted many in the past. If this were the case, then some of those I had corrupted in the past would now realise that I gave them bad advice in their youth. Thus they would be coming forward to denounce and punish me. Or if they did not want to do this themselves, members of their families – their fathers and brothers and other close relatives – would recall the harm that I had done, and act on their behalf.... Yet in fact you will find that they are all prepared to help me – the one accused of being an evil genius by Meletus and Anytus. The actual victims of my corrupting influence might be expected to help me. But as far as their mature relatives are concerned, who are uncorrupted, what other reason can they have for helping me than to defend truth and justice?

JUSTICE AND OBEDIENCE

———◆———

from *Crito* (50a–51c)

Suppose that, as I was preparing to run away from here, the Laws and Community of Athens were to come and confront us with these questions: 'Socrates, what are you intending to do? Is it not obvious that, by this escape you are planning, you are intending to the best of your ability to undermine us, the Laws, and thence destroy civic order? Do you imagine that a city can continue to exist, and not be reduced to chaos, if the legal judgments which its authorities pass are flouted and nullified by private individuals?' How should I answer such questions, and others like them? It could be argued, especially by someone skilled in rhetoric, that a bad law, leading to unjust judgments, should not be binding. So shall I reply: 'The city authorities are guilty of passing a wrong judgment against me at my trial, and thus perpetrating an injustice.' Is that to be my answer?

But then the Laws may ask: 'Was there a provision in your commitment to us as a citizen, that you could defy any judgments you disliked? Or did you agree to abide by whatever judgment the city authorities pronounced?' If I were to express astonishment at such a question, they would probably say: 'Do not be surprised, Socrates, but answer our questions – after all, you are accustomed to the process of question and answer. Tell us, what charge are you bringing against us and the city authorities, that justifies you in trying to undermine us? Did we not give you life in the first place? Was it not through us that your father married your mother, and brought you into this world? Tell us, do you complain against those of our Laws which institute marriage?' 'No, I do not,' I would reply. 'Well, do you complain against the Laws which ensure that children are brought up and educated well, as you were? Are you not grateful to those of our Laws which had charge of this, requiring your father to provide you with tuition in music and gymnastics?' 'Yes,' I would say. 'Very well. Thus, since you have been born, brought up and educated under our supervision, can you deny that you belong to us – that you and your ancestors are our children and slaves? And if this is so, do you suppose that your rights and ours are equal; and that whatever we try to do to you, you are justified in retaliating?'

The Laws would then point out: 'You do not have equality of rights with your father or your teacher, enabling you to retaliate. Nor were you allowed to answer back when you were scolded. Nor were you allowed to hit back when you were beaten. Nor were you permitted to do a great many things of this kind.

So do you think you should be allowed to defy your country and its laws? When we try to put you to death in the belief that this is just, will you respond by trying to undermine us and your country? And will you, a true devotee of goodness, claim that you are justified in doing so? In your great wisdom have you forgotten that, compared with your father and mother and all the rest of your ancestors, your country is far more precious, more venerable, more sacred, and held in greater honour both among gods and among all reasonable people? Do you not realise that you have an even greater duty to respect and assuage the anger of your country than your father's anger? Do you not see that, if you cannot persuade your country to act differently, you must simply obey its orders, submitting patiently to whatever punishment it imposes, whether it be death, flogging or imprisonment? Similarly if a country orders its citizens to go to war, risking injury and death, they must and should comply – they must not retreat or abandon their positions. Both in war and in the law courts, and indeed in every other sphere, people must do whatever their city and country commands, or else persuade their city and country that their course is just. But, as violence against parents is an unholy act, defiance of country is a far greater sin.' This is how the Laws would speak. Do you not agree that their words would be true?

THE PHILOSOPHY OF DEATH

from *Phaedo* (63b–85b)

When I die, I expect to enter the company of many wise and good gods, and also human beings who are better than those at present in this world. If I did not have this expectation, I would grieve at the imminent prospect of death. But with this expectation I would be foolish to grieve. And, although I am not utterly certain of this, I expect to meet divine masters who are supremely good....

I want to emphasise that it is quite natural for a man who has devoted his life to philosophy to feel confident in the face of death. He is hopeful of winning the greatest of all prizes in the next world after he has died. Let me make clear to you how this can be so. Ordinary people do not seem to realise that those who really apply themselves – freely and in the right manner – to philosophy are actually preparing themselves for dying and death. So, since they have been looking forward to death throughout their lives, it would obviously be absurd to be troubled when death comes.

In any line of inquiry you will attain more knowledge in proportion to the care and precision of your study. And to attain pure knowledge you must approach each subject with your Intellect; you must not let sight or any other sense interfere with your thoughts. Those who pursue knowledge by applying clear and unadulterated thought to each pure and unadulterated subject, cutting themselves off as far as possible from their eyes and ears and the rest of their bodies, will reach the goal of reality. The body prevents the soul from perceiving the truth in its fullness.... So long as we allow the body to contaminate the soul, we can never attain a complete understanding of the truth. In pursuit of sustenance, and in resisting the diseases which constantly attack it, the body never ceases to distract the soul. In addition, the body fills us with all sorts of wishes, desires, fears and all kinds of other foolish feelings, with the result that we hardly have an opportunity to think about matters of substance. Worse still, the body and its desires lead to wars, revolutions and battles. All wars are waged for the acquisition of wealth; and the reason why we want to acquire wealth is to satisfy the body – since we are slaves in its service. For all those reasons we have so little time for philosophy. Worst of all, if we do obtain any leisure from the body's claims, and turn to some line of inquiry, the body intrudes once more into our investigations; it interrupts, disturbs, and upsets the soul, preventing us from getting even a glimpse of the truth.

We must conclude, then, that if we are ever to have pure knowledge of anything, we must rid ourselves of the body, violating the soul, so the soul can contemplate things in isolation. This argument leads us to think that the wisdom we desire, and upon which we claim to have set our hearts, will be attainable only when we are dead, and not during our lifetime on earth. If pure knowledge is impossible when the soul is still tied to the body, then either it is totally impossible to acquire knowledge, or it is only possible after death – because only after death will the soul be completely isolated and independent from the body, except where this is absolutely necessary. Rather than letting ourselves be infected by the body's nature, we should purify ourselves from it until God finally delivers us from it. By keeping ourselves untainted by the follies of the body, we shall, in company with others like ourselves, gain direct access to knowledge that is pure and undefiled – that is, to truth. It would be a breach of the divine order for someone who is not pure to enter the realm of purity....

It follows that true philosophers make dying their profession; so to them, above all people, death is not in the least alarming. Look at it this way. If they are thoroughly dissatisfied with the body, and yearn to isolate the soul from it, it would be wholly unreasonable to panic or become angry at the imminent prospect of this isolation. Surely they should rejoice to be setting out at last to the place where they can attain their lifelong desire, which is wisdom, and free themselves from an association which they abhor. There are many people who have freely chosen to follow dead loved ones to the next world, in the hope of being reunited with them there. In the same way true lovers of wisdom, who have firmly understood that the only place to attain wisdom is the next world, cannot possibly be grieved at dying. On the contrary, they will be glad to make that journey. Indeed, whether people possess such an attitude is the test of whether they are genuine philosophers; only a genuine philosopher will firmly believe that entry to the next world is the route to pure wisdom. Thus the genuine philosopher cannot be afraid of death....

Let me explain further. All those who seek wisdom know that, until the time when it becomes absorbed in philosophy, the soul is a helpless prisoner. It is chained hand and foot to the body, compelled to view reality not directly, but through its prison bars. The soul wallows in utter ignorance. Philosophy can discern the ingenuity of the imprisonment: the prisoners are incarcerated by their own active desires – they are accomplices in their own confinement. Philosophy takes over the soul in this condition, and tries to set it free by gentle persuasion.

She points out that observation by means of the eyes and ears and all the other senses is fraught with deception. She thus urges the soul to refrain from using the senses unless absolutely necessary, and encourages the soul to act in isolation. The soul should trust nothing but its own isolated judgments, contemplating realities in isolation; and it should attribute no truth to judgments reached in other ways. The soul is aware of the world as it is known through the senses; but the soul's knowledge comes through the intellect, and is invisible. The soul of the true philosopher feels that it must make every effort to escape from the prison.

Thus the soul abstains as far as possible from pleasure and pain, and tries to avoid becoming upset. It reflects that giving way to pleasure, fear, pain or desire does not merely lead to some trivial misfortune, such as becoming ill or wasting money through self-indulgence; it results in some greater calamity.... Every pleasure and pain is a kind of rivet, fastening the soul to the body and pinning it down, so that the soul accepts as true whatever the body indicates. The consequence of agreeing with the body, and accepting the body's values, is that the soul cannot help acquiring the same character and interests as the body. Even at death the soul cannot break away from physical concerns to the unseen world; instead it falls back onto another body, where it takes root and grows. It cannot enter unity with that which is pure, untainted and divine.... The fear of this happening is the reason why philosophers try to detach themselves from the body....

Think of the swan. When the bird feels that it is about to die, it sings more loudly and more sweetly than it has ever sung before. It is filled with joy at the prospect of entering the presence of the god whom it has been serving. Those who think this last song is an expression of grief are quite wrong. Such people are being misled by their own fear of death, and fail to reflect that no bird sings when it is hungry or cold or distressed in any other way – not even the nightingale or swallow, whose songs are supposed to be a lament. In my opinion neither they nor the swans sing because they are sad. I believe that swans, who belong to Apollo, have prophetic powers, and sing because they know the good things that await them in the unseen world; so they are happier on their last day than they have ever been before. I consider then I am a servant of the same god as the swans, and that my prophetic powers, endowed by my god, are equal to theirs. Thus I feel no more disturbed at the prospect of leaving this world than they do.

THIS WORLD AND THE NEXT

————◆————

from *Phaedo* (109a–115a)

I believe the earth is spherical, and is surrounded by
the sky. It does not need air or any other similar force
to keep it from falling; the uniformity of the heavens
and the equilibrium of the earth itself is sufficient to
support it. Any body in equilibrium, if it is set in the
midst of a uniform medium, will have no tendency to
sink, rise or move sideways, because the equal
impulses on all sides will keep it suspended.

I also believe that the earth is vast. Those of us
who live between the eastern edge of the Black Sea
and the western edge of the Mediterranean inhabit
only a tiny proportion of the earth. We cluster round
the sea like ants and frogs round a swamp; and there
are many other peoples inhabiting similar regions
elsewhere. There are numerous hollow places all
round the earth, places of every shape and size, into
which water, mist and air have collected. But the
earth's true surface is as pure as the starry heavens
above it; and this is called 'ether' by most of our
scientific authorities. The water, mist and air are the
dregs of this ether which are continually draining
into the hollow places in the earth. We do not realise

that we are living in the hollows, but assume we are living on the top of the earth. In this respect we are like creatures in the sea itself: they may think that they are living on the surface; and seeing the sun, moon and stars through the water, they may think that the sea is the sky....

The true surface of the earth, when viewed from above, is supposed to look like a ball made from twelve pieces of skin, each piece a different colour. The colours which we know – the colours which artists use – only give a hint of these colours; they are far brighter and purer than we can imagine. One section is a wonderfully beautiful purple, another is golden; the white section is whiter than chalk or snow; the rest is made up of other colours, each more lovely than the last. Even the hollows of the earth in which humans live, filled with air and water, assume a kind of hue which comes from the reflections of the colours all around. Thus there appears to be one continuous patchwork of colours. The trees, flowers and fruits which grow on this beautiful earth are equally lovely. The mountains are also beautiful; the rocks appear smooth and opaque, revealing deep, subtle shades. The stones which are so highly prized in our world – jaspers, rubies, emeralds and the rest – are fragments of these rocks; but looked at from above, every rock is as beautiful as these fragments....

There are many kinds of creatures visible on the

earth. Some live inland, far away from the sea. Some, including humans, live on land just above and next to the sea, surrounded by air. Some live on islands with the sea on all sides. Some live high up, just above the air: as water and sea are to us, air is to them; and as air is to us, ether is to them. The climate above the air is so temperate that these creatures are free of disease, and live much longer than creatures here. And in sight, hearing, understanding and all the other faculties, they are far superior to us; as air is clearer than water, and ether clearer than air, so their faculties are clearer than ours. They have sanctuaries and temples in which the gods truly reside. And they can encounter the gods' faces, receiving oracles, prophecies, visions and all forms of divine communication. They see the sun, moon and stars as they really are; and the rest of their happiness matches the glory before their eyes.

This is the nature of the earth as a whole, and of the things which surround it. Among the hollow regions of the earth, some are deeper and more extensive than the one in which we live; some are deeper than our own region, but less extensive; and some are shallower than ours and broader. All these hollow regions are joined together underground by many connecting channels, some narrower and some wider, through which large amounts of water flow from one region to another. Some of these vast, unceasing subterranean rivers carry hot water, while some carry cold; some carry fire; some carry clear mud, while some like those in Sicily carry murky mud made from lava; some carry love itself. These various rivers constantly replenish the hollow regions. Their movement is caused by an oscillation inside the earth; and the cause of this oscillation can be explained.

One of the cavities in the earth is larger than the rest, and pierces the earth from one side to the other. The poet has spoken of it as the 'earth's deepest chasm'; and it has been given the name Tartarus. Into this great gulf all the rivers flow; and they also flow out of it. Each river acquires the nature of that part of the earth through which it flows. This great mass of liquid has no bottom or foundation, so it oscillates and surges to and fro; and the air above it does the same, accompanying the liquid as it rushes from one end of the earth to the other. Among these many and varied mighty rivers, there are four of particular importance. The greatest of these, which circumscribes the earth, is called Oceanus. Flowing in the opposite direction is Acheron, which passes through many desolate regions, and goes underground to the Acherusian Lake, where the souls of the dead mostly come; and after staying for a pre-determined period – for some it is shorter and for others it is longer – they are sent out again to be re-born as living creatures. Between Oceanus and Acheron a third river flows; and its source is a boiling lake of muddy water greater than the Mediterranean Sea, with sheets of fire burning all around it. The water coming from the lake is thick and sticky, and it takes a circular course around the inside of the earth until it reaches the edge of the Acherusian Lake. But it does not mingle with the lake; and after going round the lake many times, it plunges into the central river, Tartarus, at the lowest point. This third river is called Pyriphlegethon; and here and there across the earth it pierces through the surface with flaming jets of molten lava. Directly opposite the fourth river emerges. It first enters a wild and terrifying area, coloured leaden grey, named the Styxian region; and it flows into a lake called Styx. It acquires mysterious powers in the waters of the Styx. The river now passes underground, following a spiral course contrary to that of Pyriphlegethon. The poets call this fourth river Cocytus.

I have now described the geography of the world. The souls of those who have just died are conducted by their guardian spirits to a place of judgment. Their lives are examined to see which have been good and holy, and which have not.

Some are judged to have led neutral lives; they are taken by ships, which are waiting for them, to Acheron. There they are purified, according to what they deserve. Thus they are punished for the sins they have committed, and thereby absolved; and they are rewarded for their good deeds. Some are judged to have committed such great sins that they are incurable. These are people who are guilty of gross acts of sacrilege, of cruel and wicked murders, and similar crimes. They are punished by being hurled into Tartarus, from which they never emerge.

Some are judged to be sinners who, despite their guilt, are curable. They may have been violent to their parents in a fit of passion, and then spent the rest of their lives repenting; or they have committed some kind of manslaughter. They too must be thrown into Tartarus. But when this has been done and they have remained there for a year, the surge of the waters tosses them out. Those guilty of manslaughter go down Cocytus, while those who have harmed their parents go down Pyriphlegethon. And when they are swept past the Acherusian Lake, they cry out to those whom they have killed or violently abused, begging to be allowed to pass from the river to the lake; they plead with their victims to welcome them. If their pleas are successful, they leave the river, and their suffering is ended. But if not, they are swept away back towards Tartarus; and they continue to suffer until they can persuade their victims to relent. This is the punishment which their judge has deemed appropriate for them.

But those who are judged to have been

exceptionally holy are immediately released and set free from their present imprisonment; they move upwards, and live on the earth's surface. Some of these holy people have attained such a degree of purity through philosophy, that they can live without bodies. This enables them to progress to regions whose beauty is virtually impossible to describe, and besides, I do not have time to try.

The conclusion which any rational person on earth should draw is obvious. Every effort should be made in this life to attain some measure of goodness and wisdom. The prize is glorious and the hope is great.

Of course, no reasonable person should accept that the facts are exactly as I have described them. But something very similar is a true account of what happens to our souls after death. And regardless of the details, there is ample evidence that the soul is immortal. So it is sensible to conduct one's life on the assumption that what I say is true. Taking such a risk is noble and worthy. We should use accounts such as the one I have given as a source of encouragement; that is why I have drawn it out so long.

So let people abandon bodily pleasures and vanities, regarding them as foreign to their true purpose, and likely to do more harm than good. Let them devote themselves to the joy of acquiring knowledge, and to adorning their souls not with borrowed beauty, but with its own virtues – self-control, goodness, courage, generosity and truth. Then they can be confident about the fate of their souls; they can await calmly their journey to the next world.

THE DEATH OF SOCRATES

from *Phaedo* (115b–118a)

When Socrates had finished speaking, Crito, his companion, asked: 'Do you have directions to give to me and others about your children, or other matters? How can we best please you?'

'I have no new directions,' Socrates answered; 'I just want you to fulfil those I have already given you. If you look after your own well-being then whatever you do will please me and my children, as well as yourselves – even if you do not agree now. But if you neglect your own well-being, and fail to follow the path through life that we have been speaking about, it will do no good at all – even if you fervently agree with me now.'

'We shall be keen to do as you say,' said Crito. 'But how do you want us to bury you?'

'In whatever way you like,' replied Socrates; 'but that is if you catch me, and I don't slip through your fingers.' He laughed gently as he spoke. Then he turned to the whole group, and continued: 'I cannot persuade Crito that I am still Socrates, and that I am still talking to you and debating with you. He thinks I am already the corpse which he will soon see; and he asks how he should bury me! I have explained fully and at great length that, when I have drunk the poison, I will no longer be with you, but will depart to the happy world which belongs to the blessed. But, although I console both you and myself, my words seem to be wasted on him. You must give an assurance to Crito on my behalf – the opposite of the one which he gave to the court at my trial. He promised that I would stay, and not escape; but you must tell him that when I am dead I shall not stay – I will depart, and be gone forever. This will help Crito bear my death more easily. It will stop him becoming distressed on my account when he sees my body being burned or buried, as if something dreadful were happening to me; it will also prevent him at the funeral from referring to the body which is laid out, carried to the grave and buried as Socrates. My dear friend Crito, you must believe me that wrong statements do not merely jar on the ears hearing them, but also have a bad effect on the soul. No, you must keep up your spirits, and remind yourself that it is only my body you are burying. You can bury it as you please, in whatever way you think proper.'

With these words Socrates rose, and went into another room to bathe. Crito followed him, but told the rest of the group to wait. We discussed and reflected on what Socrates had said, and also talked about the terrible calamity that was now befalling us.

We felt as though we were losing a father, that we would be orphans for the rest of our lives. Meanwhile, when Socrates had finished bathing, his children were brought to see him; he had three sons, two very young, and one older. Also the women of his household arrived. He talked to the women and children in Crito's presence, telling them his wishes. Then he asked them to leave, and he returned to us.

He had spent a long time in the bath, making himself fresh, so it was now almost sunset. He came and sat down in our midst. He had been talking only for a few minutes when the prison officer came in, and walked up to him. 'I know,' said the officer, 'that I shall have no trouble with you, as I do with others. You will not get angry with me or curse when I carry out the court's orders, telling you to drink the hemlock. During these recent weeks I have come to recognise you are the noblest, gentlest and bravest man that has been here. You are angry with the people in court, not with me, because you realise who is responsible for your fate. I am sure you know why I have come now: it is to wish you good-bye, and to pray that you will bear your penalty well.' As he spoke, he burst into tears; and when he had finished, he turned to go away.

Socrates looked up at the officer, and said: 'Goodbye to you too. I will do as you say.' Then he spoke to the group: 'What a charming man!

Throughout my time here he has visited me, often engaging me in discussion, and shown me great kindness. How generous of him now to shed tears at my departure! But come, Crito, let us do as he requires. If the poison has been prepared, bring it in. If not, tell someone to prepare it now.'

'But surely, Socrates,' pleaded Crito, 'the sun has not yet set; it is still on the mountains. Besides, I know of other cases when the condemned man has dinner and enjoys his wine. And sometimes the man's friends continue to talk with him long after the prison officer has given the order. They delay drinking the poison until quite late at night. Please do not hurry; there is still plenty of time.'

'It is understandable that the people of whom you speak should act in that way, Crito,' said Socrates, 'because they think that they gain by it. And it is equally understandable that I should not act like that. I believe that I would gain nothing by drinking the poison a little later. I would lose respect in my own eyes if I clasped and clung to life when it has no more to offer. Come, do as I ask, and stop your objections.'

At this Crito made a sign to his slave, who was standing nearby. The slave went out, and after some time returned with the man who was to administer the poison; the man who was carrying the poison had already prepared it in a cup. 'My good fellow,' Socrates said when he saw him, 'you are an expert in these matters. Tell me what I should do.' 'Just drink it,' the man replied, 'and walk about until you feel your legs becoming heavy. At that point you should lie down; the poison will then take effect of its own accord.'

The man handed Socrates the cup. Socrates received it quite cheerfully, without any tremor or change of colour and expression. He then looked up at the man with his usual steady gaze, and asked: 'What would you say about my pouring a libation from this drink? Is that allowed, or not?' 'We only prepare what is regarded as a normal dose, Socrates,' the man replied.

'I understand,' said Socrates. 'But I presume I am allowed, or rather bound, to ask the gods that my journey from this world to the next may be pleasant. That is my prayer; and I hope it may be granted.' With no sign of emotion or distaste he then drank the poison in a single draught.

Until this moment most of the group had been successful in keeping back their tears. But as they watched him drink, and saw him drain the cup, they could restrain themselves no longer. They felt so broken-hearted that tears flooded out, and they covered their faces. They wept not for Socrates but for themselves, at the pain of losing such a friend. Crito was the first to start crying; and, when he realised that he could not hold back his tears, he left the room. But Apollodorus, who was already weeping quietly, let out such a passionate cry that the rest of the group broke down too.

But Socrates remained calm. 'Really, my friends,' he said. 'What a way to behave! My main reason for sending the women away was to prevent this kind of display. I am told that I should die in reverent silence. So control yourselves and be brave.'

The members of the group now felt ashamed, and managed to stop crying. Socrates walked about. After a time he said that his legs were heavy, so he lay down on his back, as the man who had administered the poison had instructed. The man sat near to Socrates, and examined his feet and legs. He pinched his foot hard, and asked Socrates if he felt it. Socrates said no. Then the man pinched his legs; and gradually he moved up the body, pinching each part in turn, to check that he was becoming cold and numb. He said that when the poison reached his heart, Socrates would be gone.

When he had lain down, Socrates had covered his face. But as the numbness had come up to his waist, he uncovered his face and said: 'Crito, we ought to offer a cock to the god Asclepius. See that you do it. Don't forget.' These were his last words. 'I won't forget,' replied Crito: 'it shall be done. Are you sure there is nothing else?' Socrates made no answer. But after a little while he stirred. The man uncovered him,